IT'S INCREDIBLE

HOW MUCH WE DON'T

KNOW ABOUT OUR

GRANDPARENTS!

THANKFULLY,

YOU CAN NOW SAVE

GRANDAD'S PRICELESS STORY

IN WHAT WILL BECOME

A

CHERISHED FAMILY HEIRLOOM

ASK YOUR OWN

PERSONAL QUESTIONS

OR USE QUESTIONS

FROM THE HUGE LIST

INCLUDED

AT THE

BACK OF THE BOOK

If you like the book please
consider leaving a review!

THIS
IS THE
STORY OF

QUESTION 1

GRANDAD'S ANSWER

QUESTION 2

GRANDAD'S ANSWER

QUESTION 3

GRANDAD'S ANSWER

QUESTION 4

GRANDAD’S ANSWER

QUESTION 5

GRANDAD'S ANSWER

QUESTION 6

GRANDAD'S ANSWER

QUESTION 7

GRANDAD'S ANSWER

QUESTION 8

GRANDAD'S ANSWER

QUESTION 9

GRANDAD'S ANSWER

QUESTION 10

GRANDAD'S ANSWER

QUESTION 11

GRANDAD'S ANSWER

QUESTION 12

GRANDAD'S ANSWER

QUESTION 13

GRANDAD'S ANSWER

QUESTION 14

GRANDAD'S ANSWER

QUESTION 15

GRANDAD'S ANSWER

QUESTION 16

GRANDAD'S ANSWER

QUESTION 17

GRANDAD'S ANSWER

QUESTION 18

GRANDAD'S ANSWER

QUESTION 19

GRANDAD'S ANSWER

QUESTION 20

GRANDAD'S ANSWER

QUESTION 21

GRANDAD'S ANSWER

QUESTION 22

GRANDAD'S ANSWER

QUESTION 23

GRANDAD'S ANSWER

QUESTION 24

GRANDAD'S ANSWER

QUESTION 25

GRANDAD'S ANSWER

QUESTION 26

GRANDAD'S ANSWER

QUESTION 27

GRANDAD'S ANSWER

QUESTION 28

GRANDAD'S ANSWER

QUESTION 29

GRANDAD'S ANSWER

QUESTION 30

GRANDAD'S ANSWER

QUESTION 31

GRANDAD'S ANSWER

QUESTION 32

GRANDAD'S ANSWER

QUESTION 33

GRANDAD'S ANSWER

QUESTION 34

GRANDAD'S ANSWER

QUESTION 35

GRANDAD'S ANSWER

QUESTION 36

GRANDAD'S ANSWER

QUESTION 37

GRANDAD'S ANSWER

QUESTION 38

GRANDAD'S ANSWER

QUESTION 39

GRANDAD'S ANSWER

QUESTION 40

GRANDAD'S ANSWER

QUESTION 41

GRANDAD'S ANSWER

QUESTION 42

GRANDAD'S ANSWER

QUESTION 43

GRANDAD'S ANSWER

QUESTION 44

GRANDAD'S ANSWER

QUESTION 45

GRANDAD'S ANSWER

QUESTION 46

GRANDAD'S ANSWER

QUESTION 47

GRANDAD'S ANSWER

QUESTION 48

GRANDAD'S ANSWER

QUESTION 49

GRANDAD'S ANSWER

QUESTION 50

GRANDAD'S ANSWER

QUESTION 51

GRANDAD'S ANSWER

QUESTION 52

GRANDAD'S ANSWER

QUESTION 53

GRANDAD'S ANSWER

QUESTION 54

GRANDAD'S ANSWER

QUESTION 55

GRANDAD'S ANSWER

QUESTION 56

GRANDAD'S ANSWER

QUESTION 57

GRANDAD'S ANSWER

QUESTION 58

GRANDAD'S ANSWER

QUESTION 59

GRANDAD'S ANSWER

QUESTION 60

GRANDAD'S ANSWER

QUESTION 61

GRANDAD'S ANSWER

QUESTION 62

GRANDAD'S ANSWER

QUESTION 63

GRANDAD'S ANSWER

QUESTION 64

GRANDAD'S ANSWER

QUESTION 65

GRANDAD'S ANSWER

QUESTION 66

GRANDAD'S ANSWER

QUESTION 67

GRANDAD'S ANSWER

QUESTION 68

GRANDAD'S ANSWER

QUESTION 69

GRANDAD'S ANSWER

QUESTION 70

GRANDAD'S ANSWER

QUESTION 71

GRANDAD'S ANSWER

QUESTION 72

GRANDAD’S ANSWER

QUESTION 73

GRANDAD'S ANSWER

QUESTION 74

GRANDAD'S ANSWER

QUESTION 75

GRANDAD'S ANSWER

QUESTION 76

GRANDAD'S ANSWER

QUESTION 77

GRANDAD'S ANSWER

QUESTION 78

GRANDAD'S ANSWER

QUESTION 79

GRANDAD'S ANSWER

QUESTION 80

GRANDAD'S ANSWER

QUESTION 81

GRANDAD’S ANSWER

QUESTION 82

GRANDAD'S ANSWER

QUESTION 83

GRANDAD'S ANSWER

QUESTION 84

GRANDAD'S ANSWER

QUESTION 85

GRANDAD'S ANSWER

QUESTION 86

GRANDAD'S ANSWER

QUESTION 87

GRANDAD'S ANSWER

QUESTION 88

GRANDAD'S ANSWER

QUESTION 89

GRANDAD'S ANSWER

QUESTION 90

GRANDAD'S ANSWER

QUESTION 91

GRANDAD'S ANSWER

QUESTION 92

GRANDAD'S ANSWER

QUESTION 93

GRANDAD'S ANSWER

QUESTION 94

GRANDAD'S ANSWER

QUESTION 95

GRANDAD'S ANSWER

QUESTION 96

GRANDAD'S ANSWER

QUESTION 97

GRANDAD'S ANSWER

QUESTION 98

GRANDAD'S ANSWER

QUESTION 99

GRANDAD'S ANSWER

QUESTION 100

GRANDAD'S ANSWER

QUESTION 101

GRANDAD'S ANSWER

QUESTION IDEAS

- What is the funniest thing you remember from your childhood?
- If you could be anyone for the day, who would you be?
- What's something you've never done that you'd still love to try?
- If you had a million dollars, what would you spend it on?
- What's the thing that makes you happiest when you think about your life?
- What's the most important piece of advice anyone ever gave you and why?
- Have you owned any pets?
- How did you choose the names you wanted to give your children?
- Do you know how to play any musical instruments?
- Do you have anything special that's been passed down the generations?
- What important world event do you best remember?
- Describe your perfect day!
- How did you travel when you were young?
- If you could ask anyone in the world a question, who would it be and what would you ask?
- What are you thankful for?

QUESTION IDEAS

- What's the biggest lesson you've learned from life?
- What were your grandmother and grandfather like?
- What's the kindest thing you've ever done for someone?
- Where were you born?
- Were you named after a family member or does your name have a special meaning?
- Were you ever punished by your parents for being naughty?
- What did you want to be when you were young?
- What is the most important lesson that your parents taught you?
- Did you get an allowance? How much was it and what did you spend your money on?
- Did you ever get in trouble as a child or teenager?
- How did you meet Granny?
- Where was your wedding?
- What was your first job?
- If you were going to be quoted in a book of good advice, what would you say?
- Where does your name come from and why were you called that?

QUESTION IDEAS

- Do you still have anything that was given to you by your parents or grandparents?
- Do you have any popular family recipes?
- What's the thing that's changed the most about the world since you were born?
- What's the best invention you've seen?
- What do you wish people today would learn from history?
- If you had a phone that could call the past, who would you ring and why?
- What's your most treasured memory with each of your parents?
- What jobs did your parents do?
- Are there any fun family legends and stories about people from older generations?
- Do you have any old photos of other family members?
- What games did you like playing when you were a child?
- What was school like when you were young?
- Did you have a hobby or did you collect anything?
- What is the best city to visit?

QUESTION IDEAS

- What countries have you been to?
- Where have you lived? Tell me about your first house.
- What foods did you like best as a kid?
- How did your parents choose your name? Did you have any nicknames?
- When and where were you born?
- Did you like to play sports?
- What was your first job?
- What did you do after high school — go to college, get a job?
- What do you remember most about your wedding day?
- Looking back at your life, what are you most proud of?
- What do you want your children and grandchildren to remember about you?
- If you could have one superpower, what would it be and why?
- If you could take three things with you on a desert island, what items would you choose?
- What is your best advice to give your grandchildren?
- What is the most valuable thing you learned from your parents?
- At what age did you retire?

QUESTION IDEAS

- What was the funniest thing my mom/dad did as a child?
- Has our family always lived in this country?
- Does anyone in our family speak another language?
- What do you most wish children growing up now could experience from your own childhood?
- What's your first ever memory?
- Did you have any chores to do? What were they?
- Did you have a nickname or give anyone else one? What was it and how did you get it?
- How did your family spend time together when you were young?
- What did your friends do for fun when you were young?
- Did you have a curfew and what time was it? Did you ever miss curfew?
- Who was your best man at your wedding
- What is your most treasured memory with your children?
- What makes you happy?

QUESTION IDEAS

- What was your house like as a child?
- What was your best subject at school?
- Which teacher did you like best in school?
- What was your best friends name?
- Do you have a nickname that your siblings or friends call you?
- How did you get your nickname?
- What's your biggest accomplishment?
- What's been the biggest surprise about the way your life has gone?
- What's the best thing that's ever happened in your life?
- How many jobs have you had?
- What are some fun stories about you and your friends from when you were younger?
- Who or what changed your life the most?
- What's the best place you've ever been on vacation?
- Is there anyone you've lost touch with who you wish you could find again?
- What was the worst trouble you ever got into?
- What is the best thing about being a grandparent?
- What were your grandparents like?

Printed in Great Britain
by Amazon

20707419R00063